D0122291

negotiation

Brief Lessons and Inspiring Stories

A book to inspire and celebrate
your achievements.

By Jim Williamson

Edited by Dan Zadra
Designed by Kobi Yamada and Steve Potter
Compendium Inc.

DEDICATION

This book is dedicated to the mentors who guided me; the sales managers who challenged me; the clients who trusted me; the students who followed me; the colleagues who teamed with me; the partners who dreamed with me; and to my wife, Maxine, who believed in me.

ACKNOWLEDGEMENTS

The author and editors sincerely appreciate the following people who contributed invaluable assistance, spirit or content to Lessons Learned: John Becvar, Delores Bergstrom, Dick Beselin, Ron Butler, Tom Black, Steve Cheney, Debbie Cottrell, Ron Crawford, Don Daniels, Curt Dickerson, Cris Dippel, Don Dougherty, Ron Fox, David Haines, Elaine Harwell, Denny Holm, Kelly Holm, Cheryl Hungate, Dick Iversen, Gary Jacobson, Eric Jonson, Harry Mandros, Mark Matteson, Bob Moawad, John Moeller, Anna Nerbovig, Pat O'Day, Vince Pfaff, Dennis Schmahl, Janet Scroggs, Jack Sparacio, Dave Sund, Larry Sund, Ron Tarrant, Greg Tiemann, Lee Tillman, Don Williamson, and Dan Zadra.

WITH SPECIAL THANKS TO

Suzanne Hoonan, President, Advantage Learning, without whose creativity and guidance this book would still be merely a good idea.

CREDITS

Edited by Dan Zadra

Designed by Kobi Yamada and Steve Potter

ISBN: 1-888-387-74-2

TABLE OF CONTENTS

INTRODUCTION

All life is a negotiation.
—Wendy Wasserstein

Many people feel that "negotiation" has little relevance to them. The truth is, life is an endless succession of agreements (or disagreements). Children bargain with their parents, doctors with their patients, salespeople with their customers or vendors, employees with their managers, and some with the IRS. Oh yes, and we all negotiate with our spouses and partners. In fact, Reverend Dale Turner suggests that the standard wedding vow should be changed to "love, honor and negotiate."

This is not a book of negotiating "tricks" or "weapons." If your goal is to intimidate or manipulate the other party—to cream them or kill them—this book is not for you. My idea of a tough negotiator is not someone who is cunning enough to make one party lose or feel bad—it's someone who is big enough and wise enough to help both parties win and feel good. That's the kind of insights and ideas you'll find in these pages.

It always makes me happy to see an attorney sign up for our Negotiation workshops. If you think about it, every lawyer is formally trained to handle an adversarial relationship, but not every lawyer is formally trained to negotiate a Win/Win relationship. If you're like me, you don't really want to negotiate a short-term victory that ends up in court or makes an enemy for life. You want a mutual resolution that not only stays resolved but ensures that you've won a friend or customer for life.

I'll never forget the first time I visited the World Trade Center's observation decks. An inspiring historical display, dating all the way back to the fifth century BC, showed how different cultures have traded and bartered in peace through the ages. Inscribed above the display for all the world to see were the words, "Early Negotiations." Ironically, that inscription is gone, now, lost in the rubble. But the spirit of peaceful bargaining and collaborative negotiation lives on and cannot be extinguished.

Jim Williamson

—Jim Williamson

COMPASS POINTS

*If you don't know where you're going,
you might wind up someplace else.*

—Yogi Berra

To ensure that you get the greatest possible value from this book, please take a few quiet minutes to complete the following reflective thinking exercise. A similar exercise is included at the end of the book.

1. My greatest strength in negotiating with people:

_____

_____

2. One negotiation situation I'd like to handle better:

_____

_____

3. The person whose negotiation ability I most admire:

_____

4. The one quality (or qualities) I most admire about him or her:

_____

_____

5. If I get nothing else from this book, I'm going to keep an open mind and look for ways to improve the following

_____

_____

A BOOK TO
INSPIRE AND CELEBRATE
YOUR ACHIEVEMENTS

INK IT

Oh, the difference between
right and almost right.

—Don Lutz

The keynote speaker at a negotiation conference was introduced this way: "Please give a warm welcome to one of the top financial planners in the nation—a man who made his first million at age 22 by investing in oil futures."

Stepping to the podium, the speaker smiled sheepishly and said, "Thanks for the kind introduction, but I need to correct a couple points. Actually, it wasn't me—it was my older brother who made that particular investment. And he wasn't 22, he was 32. And he didn't invest in oil futures, he invested in gold futures. And it wasn't a million dollars, it was five million. And he didn't make it—he *lost* it."

The point of the story is that one or two words can often mean a huge swing in the fortunes of life or the outcome of a negotiation. What did you *really* hear? Did your boss say he was giving you a "day off"…or did he say you were having an "off day?" Big difference.

The rule of thumb is simple: As you move forward in a negotiation, write down the points of agreement immediately as they are agreed-upon. Don't just think it—*ink it!* At the conclusion, quickly review each point together with the other party, verifying accuracy and intent. Have both parties initial each point as you move down the list, and then agree that one or both of you will take accountability for converting it into a final agreement.

I believe in the spirit of the time-honored "Gentleman's Agreement." But they always seem to go better when there are a few handwritten notes to refresh everyone's memory.

LESSONS LEARNED

- *Early on, ask permission to take notes.*
- *Review each point together to ensure mutual understanding.*
- *Assign accountability for converting notes to a formal agreement.*

DECISION MAKERS

You can't jaw with a bunch of rowdies,
it's best to find their leader.

—William "Bat" Masterson, 1873

It was true in Wichita back in the 1800's and, as far as I'm concerned, it's still true today. Given a choice, I try to avoid selling or negotiating in a group setting. I prefer instead to identify the leader or the key decision maker and then work things through, one on one.

I know this advice may fly in the face of conventional sales wisdom. My friends in the real estate industry will remind me that a home sold today to just one spouse or partner must be re-sold to both of them tomorrow. The same is true in a corporate setting. We've all had the experience of making our best presentation to the key decision maker, only to have him or her invite us back to repeat the presentation to "the team."

But I still stand by my advice: Whenever possible, try to sell and negotiate, one on one, with the key decision maker. If you're caught in a group situation, you may "think" you're playing on a level playing surface—but you actually have no way of guessing the real group dynamics. One person may show up to review the project entirely on its merits; two may show up to support the decision maker "no matter what," and three may show up to torpedo the decision maker "no matter what."

In general, I recommend that you do a good job of presenting to and negotiating with the leader—and then he or she will know the ins and outs of selling it to the rest of the team.

LESSONS LEARNED

- *Try to avoid negotiating in a group setting.*
- *Reach agreement with the decision maker.*
- *Let the leader become your emissary.*

TIGER TEAMS

The secret is to gang up on the problem,
rather than each other.

—*Thomas Stallkamp, Chrysler*

Sometimes you're the client, and sometimes you're the vendor. Most of us find ourselves in *both* roles, sometimes on the same day. Since price is such a common negotiating point for both sides, here's a great way to bring the two sides together without a squabble:

Cost versus Price: Chrysler deals with thousands of suppliers, but their "collaborative approach" will work for virtually any client/vendor relationship, large or small. Instead of wrangling with suppliers to provide one-time "price discounts," Chrysler challenges them to come up with long-term "cost-saving ideas." Unlike a discount which is temporary, a cost-saving idea is viewed by both sides as a *permanent improvement* that results in ongoing, future savings—and helps solidify the client/supplier relationship in the bargain.

Beat the Bogey: Chester Karrass teaches a similar approach called "Tiger Teams." For example, if you're a manufacturer, you might set up employee "Tiger Teams" comprised of personnel from purchasing, production and design. Together, your tigers set a cost-cutting goal—maybe fifteen percent below the current production budget—and they call it the "bogey." Then your Tiger Team members inform suppliers, "Look, this is all we can spend this year on your product or service, so we need your creative ideas on how to cut costs."

Suppliers appreciate the collaborative approach, clearly understand the limits, and willingly cooperate with your people as "part of the team" to beat the bogey. No negotiation is even necessary.

LESSONS LEARNED

- *Initiate a collaborative versus competitive approach.*
- *Collaborate on cost-saving ideas versus price discounts.*
- *Discounts are temporary; cost-saving ideas are permanent improvements.*

LABOR VS. MANAGEMENT

People tend to resist that which is
forced upon them. People tend to support
that which they help to create.

—Vince Pfaff

Somewhere I have a list of 24 items that are common points of
contention between employees and their companies. That's a
long list, but any seasoned Labor Union representative or
Human Resources director could probably provide an even
longer list. Please know that many of the 24 most hotly-
negotiated problems disappear by themselves when both
parties focus first on what they can "give," rather than what
they want to "get."

Employees at Corning's Erwin, New York plant wanted higher
wages, more job security, better training, and better working
conditions. Management, on the other hand, wanted higher
quality, better productivity, lower costs, and fewer defects.
Both sides decided to focus on how they could actually give
the other side exactly what was wanted. Instead of forcing the
same old issues on each other, they decided to create
something new together.

It took a lot of trust, but management let go of the reins and empowered the employees themselves to solve the company's problems. Employees set their own hours, worked without supervision, and made many decisions about daily operations.

Result: Defects declined from 13,000 to 600 per million, and late shipments were cut from 12 percent to one percent. To give back to their employees, Corning introduced new bonuses and profit sharing that directly rewarded the employees' own increased efficiencies. They also offered new skills training to all employees. Master a new skill that helps the company, and you receive a pay raise—simple as that. Nothing left to argue or negotiate about.

LESSONS LEARNED

- *Trust each other again and again.*
- *Focus on giving before getting.*
- *Work on creating something new—together.*

DREAMS FIRST

Start with the dream;
proceed with the plan.
—*Dr. Larry Case*

Hardball negotiators are never satisfied with enough. They always try to wring one more concession from the other party. Their favorite lament is, "I think I left some money on the table."

Connie Maguire, a financial consultant for Wells Fargo, decries this approach. "In today's environment, macho does not prove mucho," she says. "Most deals come together faster in a spirit of cooperation, not competition." I agree. One of my guiding philosophies is, "Be thrilled when the other party gets what they want, as long as you get what *you* want."

The hardball negotiator thinks, "I wonder how far I can push this guy?" The Win/Win negotiator thinks, "I wonder what his/her ideal outcome might be?" In fact, try asking the other party upfront, "What is your dream-come-true for this meeting? If you can describe it, I bet we can work backwards to reach it— or at least come close."

If you learn that the other party's dream outcome is surprisingly *less* than you were willing to offer, you can immediately fulfill their dream and get more than you originally anticipated in the bargain. If their dream outcome is about the *same* as you were willing to offer, once again you can close the deal in record time. Or, if their dream is *more* than you are willing to offer, simply use their benchmark to negotiate a mutually acceptable outcome.

Since the other party establishes the "dream outcome," there can be no more wrangling if you come close to fulfilling it. The logic becomes, "We've now achieved your ideal, so let's move forward."

LESSONS LEARNED

- *Ask the other party to describe their dream outcome upfront.*
- *Ask them to keep it reasonable, not frivolous.*
- *Work backwards from the dream and try to fulfill it.*

FACTS

*One of the highest arts of negotiation
requires the ability to smell a real fact.*
—Harold Geneen, former CEO, ITT

Most negotiations proceed from a set of facts that both sides assume to be true. Once the facts are established and accepted, every subsequent point in the negotiation will be predicated upon them. Before you begin any negotiation, adopt the habit of quietly and thoroughly exploring the validity of every assumption—and you'll likely discover that some facts aren't really facts at all.

Suppose you're negotiating a pay raise with your employer. He may remind you that your sales did not increase last year; therefore, your pay should not increase. But maybe that's not a real fact, it's a partial fact. The real fact may be that you devoted 25% of your selling time to hiring and training three new salespeople who, in turn, contributed a 40% increase in sales, over and above what you contributed.

I once negotiated a book contract with an East Coast publisher who assured me, "We guarantee the lowest printing prices in the country for books of this quality." That was a true fact. But, after analyzing that fact, I asked the publisher, "What if these books were printed *outside* the country?" It turned out that an offshore printer could do the equivalent job for 30% less—and, believe me, that new fact pleasantly impacted the outcome of our negotiations.

Harold Geneen of ITT once cautioned his managers, "We're counting on you to base your decisions on unshakable facts. Beware of unfactual facts, including apparent facts, assumed facts, reported facts, hoped-for facts, obvious conclusions and basic assumptions. Learn to tell a genuine snapping turtle from the others."

LESSONS LEARNED

- *Quietly explore the validity of every assumption.*
- *Establish the true facts upon which the negotiation will be based.*
- *Gain agreement from the other party on those facts and proceed.*

HANDOFFS

*It's not only what you know,
but who you know, that's important.*

—Old Axiom

Every negotiation is influenced by the "Two C's"—competency and chemistry. You may have highly competent people negotiating on your behalf, but if the chemistry between the two parties is bad—watch out!

Years ago my brother Don served as CFO of a consumer products company in Nashville. One year the company found itself in a complex income tax dispute with the IRS. The dispute involved the interpretation of an arcane section of the tax code. Eventually the matter reached the appellate level of the IRS in Nashville, which was led by a 65-year-old Vanderbilt educated attorney who was born and raised in Tennessee.

"This set up an interesting choice," recalls Don. "We already had an attorney in our stable who was about the same age as the IRS attorney, had grown up in Nashville, and had gone to the same University. The chemistry was bound to be great— but he lacked the competency for this particular tax issue.

"Our other choice was the national expert on the issue—a CPA from Chicago—but we worried that he might butt heads with the Southern IRS attorney. The solution? We brought them *both* to the negotiation."

Don's in-house attorney began the meeting by reminiscing with the IRS attorney about college days at Vanderbilt and Southern-style hunting trips. Then came the all-important handoff. "Charlie, I have met with this CPA from Chicago and he is all right—he knows his stuff."

The handoff sweetened the chemistry, enabling Don's expert to competently present his argument without being perceived as a "Chicago expert in a Southern court." They were given fair hearing and eventually prevailed.

LESSONS LEARNED

- *Competency is vital.*
- *Chemistry is crucial.*
- *A third party can often enhance one or both.*

PAUSE

Don't lose your head—
it's the best part of your body.

—Jimmy Snider

Rub two different points of view up against each other and there is friction. Friction causes sparks, which can lead to fire, which can quickly turn your negotiation to ashes.

I have been in routine situations where a few misspoken words hit someone's hot button, and suddenly we had a room filled with Hatfields and McCoys. Words are like bullets—and a bullet, once fired, cannot be retrieved.

My advice: If someone takes an emotional shot at you or your program, push your pause button, not your hot button. Count to 10 or take a stretch break. By maintaining your cool, you have just taken control of the high ground in this negotiation. Someone may have lost his or her head, but hopefully you have kept yours. Use the moment wisely. Help the other party save face by graciously acknowledging their anger or frustration: "I can see you're frustrated about this point, Bob, let's work through it. You'll have our full cooperation. The relationship is far more important to us than this point."

Remember: Negotiation without some type of conflict is unrealistic. Conflict can create friction and fire, but it can also create heat and light. It's all in how you handle it. An argument is always about something that has been made more important than the relationship. If you can re-focus everyone on the relationship, the argument can usually be quickly resolved. Above all, keep your temper; nobody wants it.

LESSONS LEARNED

- *Negotiation without some type of friction is unrealistic.*
- *No one thinks clearly when their fists are clenched.*
- *Push your pause button; don't say something you'll regret.*

SAME SIDE

Focus on the quality of your
long-term relationships, rather than the
quantity of your short-term transactions.
—Scott Johnson

Back in the 1980's Larry Wilson wrote a fascinating book called "Changing the Game." One of his premises: For a hundred years virtually all salespeople were men; therefore most men naturally adhered to the same time-honored selling patterns.

For example, most salesmen were taught the fine art of "overcoming objections." Simply put, if the other party expressed a concern of any kind, a good salesman always had several techniques for countering the concern. No matter what, the primary objective was to complete the transaction and make the sale.

Then, during the Seventies and Eighties, millions of women entered the workforce. Larry noted that women brought powerful new perspectives to sales—sacrilegious perspectives that would fundamentally change the rules of the game. Upon hearing a legitimate objection, for example, a female salesperson might candidly *agree* with the objection, rather then countering it. This jeopardized the immediate sale, but it also created a trusting relationship. And forming a long-term trust relationship, rather than making a short-term sale, was the primary objective.

It was almost as if the salesperson and her prospective client were on the same side. In fact studies suggest that salesmen do tend to sit on the opposite side of the table from their client, while saleswomen instinctively tend to sit on the same side.

Let the "same side" be a metaphor for your next selling situation or negotiation. Visualize yourself on the same side of the table as the other party. Try to see the negotiation, not as a contest, but as a collaboration. Competition is a time-honored tradition in negotiation—but competition isn't nearly as powerful as communication and cooperation.

LESSONS LEARNED

- *Visualize yourself on the same side.*
- *Don't sell—consult.*
- *Think "relationship" first; transaction second.*

PARAPHRASING

A great number of people think
they are communicating when they are
merely rearranging their prejudices.

—William James

Whenever two experienced parties negotiate in good faith, you usually hear lots of paraphrasing. At its best, paraphrasing is a terrific communication tool. It proves you're listening, you care, you understand—and it therefore accelerates both parties to a mutually beneficial conclusion. To paraphrase, simply restate what you think you heard in a summary format. It might sound like this: "I hear you saying that you're concerned about our timeline, but not our price. Is that right?"

There's a fine line, however, between honest paraphrasing and manipulation. I remember when Faye LaPointe, a brilliant Native American leader, publicly called the Federal Government to task during a heated negotiation. Faye always spoke in clear, elegant, straightforward sentences, and she couldn't understand why certain bureaucrats spoke in circles. One day she stood up in a meeting at our state Capitol and confronted them.

"Please explain this to me," she said politely. "When I tell you something from my heart, you take my words and parrot them back to me. But I have noticed that you sometimes twist one or two small points so you can change the overall meaning to suit yourselves. What shall we call that?"

The flustered speaker responded, "Ms. LaPointe, I was merely paraphrasing what you said." Faye shook her head sadly and replied, "I think of the past three hundred years, and it suddenly dawns on me that there is no such concept as paraphrasing in the Native American community. We don't even have a word for it."

Remember, paraphrasing is a valid way to help clarify communication, but only if it's done with sincerity, accuracy and integrity.

LESSONS LEARNED

- *High-integrity paraphrasing is a good negotiation tool.*
- *Honest, accurate feedback is the goal.*
- *Your intent should be to understand, not to manipulate.*

POSITIONS VERSUS INTERESTS

Never bargain over positions;
always bargain over underlying interests.

—*Roger Fisher and William Ury*

"**G**etting To Yes," by Fisher and Ury is one of the best books I have found on the psychology of good negotiation. The following story, adapted from that book, is a classic illustration of the critical difference between a position and an interest:

Two executives are quarreling in the conference room on a hot summer afternoon. One wants the window open; the other wants it closed. The more they bicker, the more stubborn they become about their positions.

Finally, their supervisor enters and asks manager Number One why he wants the window open. "I need fresh air," he answers. She then asks Number Two why he wants it closed. "I hate the draft," he says. The manager offers a simple solution: "Let's turn on the air conditioner which brings in twenty-five percent outside air and distributes it evenly, thereby avoiding a draft."

This story is typical of many negotiations. The supervisor could not have invented the solution if she focused only on the two men's stated positions of wanting the window open or closed. Instead she looked to their underlying and implied interests of "fresh air" and "no draft."

Remember that underlying interests motivate people; they are silent movers behind the hubbub of positions. Your position is something you've decided upon; your interests are what caused you to decide. A position is likely to be clear and explicit; an interest is likely to be unclear and implicit.

Identify the interests behind the positions and you are already halfway home to a successful negotiation.

LESSONS LEARNED

- *Recognize that underlying interests motivate people.*
- *Realize that stated positions cause both parties to "dig in."*
- *Seek out and bargain over the interest behind the position.*

UNDER GLASS

*Not everything is negotiable,
but everything is solvable.*

—Malcolm Forbes

Cliff is a jeweler specializing in fine timepieces. Cliff's watches are expensive, but connoisseurs appreciate his "rock bottom prices." *Highest quality at lowest price, guaranteed*—that's Cliff's marketing niche.

But his niche is also his problem. Most walk-in customers fully expect to negotiate a better price with a watch merchant. But Cliff can't negotiate because his prices are already "rock bottom." This situation previously resulted in hard feelings, as customers insisted on trying to wear Cliff down. Cliff finally solved the problem by placing his elegantly printed price list under a thick piece of glass at the front counter. At the top of the price list is this message: *To my valued customers: My prices are not negotiable, but for your convenience they are verifiably the best and cannot be beat. I guarantee it.*

We often hear that "everything is negotiable," but practically speaking it's not true. Whenever you have a certain item that is not up for grabs, you can save both parties time and grief. Right up front, place that particular item "under glass" (or in a clear plastic sheet protector) where the other party's pencil can't get to it. Then focus together on the items that *can* be negotiated.

The printing schedule for this book, for example, could not be accelerated. The printer's docket was maxed, so my printing date was legitimately "under glass." Since we couldn't negotiate the printing schedule, we solved it by negotiating the delivery method. Shipping my books by ground would take 10-14 days; but if the printer conceded to ship by air, it would save me a week. Done deal.

LESSONS LEARNED

- *Most things are negotiable, but not all.*
- *Upfront, put the things that aren't negotiable "under glass."*
- *Focus on those items which can be negotiated.*

ASSUMPTIONS

Most people see what is,
and never see what can be.

—*Albert Einstein*

I love boats. Over the years I've purchased several from my friend, Greg Tiemann. We know and trust each other, so the negotiations go smoothly—but not as smoothly as the sale in the following story.

As Greg tells it, the mother of all boat shows is the annual Fort Lauderdale International Boating Exhibit. People from all over the world are drawn to the event; most are dressed to the nines, and many come with checkbook in hand. The multi-language negotiations over cash sales for high-priced yachts can become heated and difficult. One sale that day, however, was incredibly simple. Ironically, it was made by a rookie broker representing the Broward Yacht display, and he snatched it right out from under the noses of his more experienced colleagues.

It was midday when a young, unshaven guy approached a gleaming 130-foot Broward. Dressed in rumpled jeans and

T-shirt, he stood out like a walnut in a string of pearls—so the other brokers left him to the rookie. Too bad, because the prospect turned out to be the CEO of one of the world's largest pizza chains and—you guessed it—he took delivery on the Broward, no muss or fuss.

My philosophy in negotiating (and life) is to "assume nothing but expect anything." Have unconditional warm regards for all people at all times, and treat everyone you meet with dignity and respect. Sure, some people may turn out to be unqualified, untrustworthy, or even dishonest. But those qualities quickly emerge in the discovery process. The best time to evaluate people is *after* you get to know them, not before.

LESSONS LEARNED

- *Assume nothing, but expect anything.*
- *Treat everyone you meet with dignity and respect.*
- *Some winners are disguised as losers, and vice versa.*

THIRD PARTY

Round and round the two men fought.
Soon they had a brilliant thought:
"Three can solve what two cannot."

—Teamsters Union jingle

When you've come to a standstill in any negotiation, large or small, Ron Crawford's advice is, "Think third party." As the Superintendent of Snohomish Public Schools, Dr. Crawford averted a disastrous teachers strike by calling in an impartial outside facilitator. The facilitator quickly built new bridges. He diplomatically helped both sides disconnect from their opposing positions, and reconnect to their mutual interests.

Dr. Crawford reminds us that third parties are everywhere and all around us. Mediators, arbitrators, referees, real estate agents, family counselors, trusted mentors, best friends, Father O'Malley, Uncle Bob, Aunt Martha, and your friendly corner bartender—all can serve as helpful intermediaries, depending on the nature of the conflict.

In divorce proceedings, a mutually acceptable counselor can often help two wounded spouses keep their attorneys at bay and their bank accounts intact. When building a home, an ego conflict between the home owner and the architect has often been resolved by a savvy contractor.

In his book, "Going For It," Victor Kiam told how he called on a unique third party to negotiate the purchase of a promising but failing apparel business. Victor generously offered $500,000, but the idealistic young owner insisted on $2 million, a ridiculous sum. Meanwhile, the business was quickly veering toward bankruptcy. Victor finally called on the young man's own bankers to resolve the impasse.

"You know the numbers," Victor told the bankers. "You care about the owner, and he trusts you. See if you can reason with him." They did, and the deal was swiftly and amicably completed.

LESSONS LEARNED

- *Impasses are common between two parties.*
- *Look to a third party to resolve them.*
- *Be sure the third party is impartial.*

DEADLINES

Negotiation is chess on caffeine.

—Anon

Master negotiators are often described as the "poker players" of the business world, but I like the chess metaphor (above) better. Chess players have many moves at their command. They think proactively, anticipating their opponent's next move, often projecting several moves ahead.

The problem with chess is that it sometimes drags on and on, and that can be a real problem with negotiation, too. In general, the longer the negotiation, the more likely the two parties will hunker down into intractable positions. During the summer of 2002, for example, Major League Baseball was well on the way to another strike. Each delay drove management and the players deeper into their bunkers. Finally, the players arbitrarily set a deadline of August 30 as a strike date. At that point both sides came to the bargaining table with a new sense of urgency, and an agreement was swiftly hammered out.

Common sense will tell you when and how to use deadlines as a strategic element in your proposals or negotiations. There's an obvious difference between "bogging down" and "rushing things." Look around for examples. The healthy pace of the real estate industry is predicated on real but reasonable closing dates. Insurance policies have thirty-day grace periods. Airlines give you 24 hours to cancel your ticket. Hotels afford you the courtesy of a reservation, but insist on enforceable check-in times. These deadlines are all reasonable. Do we resent them? Yes, sometimes. Do they change our behavior and move us to action? Absolutely!

The next time you come to the bargaining table, consider how you might build a reasonable sense of urgency into the negotiation. Think, "chess on caffeine."

LESSONS LEARNED

- *Avoid delays; keep negotiations moving to completion.*
- *Do set reasonable targets and due dates for agreements to be finalized.*
- *Use "drop–dead" deadlines, not as time ploys, but only as a last resort.*

THE FUTURE

If you eat the chicken today,
you can't have eggs tomorrow.
—*Italian Proverb*

Here is a classic negotiation story about William Wrigley, Jr., the man who launched Juicy Fruit and Wrigley's Spearmint Gum back in the 1890's. I am happy to hear that Wrigley's great-grandson, Wrigley CEO Bill Wrigley, Jr., is still weaving this story into his speeches. It says something about the core values of the company, and probably explains why the Wrigley Company has remained an industry leader for more than a hundred years.

The story goes that the owner of a small business came into Wrigley's office one day to propose a line of promotional items. Wrigley's wealth, influence and intelligence made him an imposing figure in any negotiation. Soon the deal was done, and the papers were signed on the spot. Then Wrigley noticed a look of dejection on the other man's face. "Why so glum?" asked Wrigley.

"I'm beginning to think that I shouldn't have signed that agreement," the man replied. "I will probably lose money on it."

Wrigley could've held the man's feet to the fire. After all, the prevailing business philosophy of that era was, "A deal is a deal." Instead, he tore up the agreement and said, "Let's start fresh and renegotiate. We don't want to do business with anybody who loses money on us."

Wrigley went on to purchase the Chicago Cubs, built championship teams, and developed Catalina Island into one our nation's top resort destinations. But he didn't do it alone; he did it by negotiating solid long-term "win/win" relationships. His philosophy: "Our agreements should make us friends, not enemies. They should make us better, not bitter."

LESSONS LEARNED

- *Be guided by your core values.*
- *Strive for a balanced agreement.*
- *Foster solid long-term relationships.*

HOLD YOURSELF HIGH

If you don't prize yourself, who will?
If you don't think well of yourself,
why would anyone?

—*Graham Scott*

Most of us change jobs several times in our lives. Usually it's a change for the better. The more you advance in your career, the more leverage you'll have to negotiate your compensation package. Be careful; hold yourself high. This little story from my friend Kelly Holm illustrates the point:

"Years ago a leading Seattle design firm approached me about a great position. Competition was stiff; interviews were already underway with candidates from New York, San Francisco and Los Angeles. To prepare for the interview, I researched salary ranges in both the local market and the other three cities. I went to the interview confident that a fair salary should be 20% to 45% higher than my current position. I didn't want to undersell or oversell myself—so I mentally settled on a figure in the middle.

"The good news is that the President offered me the position; the bad news is that the compensation package was nearly $15,000 *below* my target. A little voice in my head screamed, 'Take it. . .you really want this job. . .once they see you in action, they'll raise your pay!' Instead, I firmly stood my ground. We agreed to talk again the following day.

"When he called, I held my ground again. Finally, he said that he had talked it over with his partner, and they had agreed to meet my target if that's what it took. Why? Because they wanted someone who believed in his own value to be on *their* team negotiating for *their* company. If I had sold myself short, someone else would have surely won that position."

LESSONS LEARNED

- *Know your value, ask for what's fair, and stick to it.*
- *Neither undersell nor oversell.*
- *You must believe in yourself if you expect others to believe in you.*

ASK, "WHAT IF?"

There is always a way—over,
under, around or through.
—*Dan Zadra*

I love watching realtors at work. Home ownership is still the Great American Dream, and the realtor's role is to make the dream come true. If you don't have the down payment or can't agree on a price, a good realtor will think outside the box and usually find a way. It's the kind of resourcefulness that everyone should bring to any negotiation.

Northwest realtor Anna Nerbovig tells her clients, "If you have a dream, we'll do whatever it takes to make it happen." Recently two newlyweds chose a house that sorely tested Anna's philosophy. It was clearly out of the young couple's price range. After several counteroffers, thousands of dollars still separated the buyer and seller.

Undaunted, Anna asked herself, "What if?" She knew the groom had a landscaping business, and she had heard the mortgage broker remark that she wanted her own home landscaped. Anna also approached the listing agent about her landscaping needs and—*presto*—a creative solution emerged. What if the mortgage lender got her home landscaped in exchange for reducing her loan fees; what if the seller got his price as a result of the listing agent reducing her commission; what if the selling agent took a little less commission; and what if the listing agent got a rockery in her garden built courtesy of the groom? Wouldn't this result in the newlyweds landing the home of their dreams? It did!

Your resources are always far greater than you imagine. When negotiating an agreement, never wonder, "Gee, can we really put this deal together?" Ask yourself instead, "*How* can we put this deal together?"

LESSONS LEARNED

- *Explore the full scope of interests for all parties.*
- *Think outside the box; there's always a way— find it.*
- *Generate a list of possible options and then "connect the dots."*

RISK

Sometimes the only way
to hold on to something
is to let go of it.

—*Don Ward*

"It's my final offer, take it or leave it." That line is usually used as an empty ploy or, worse yet, a bullying tactic. That said, there are times when the only sane message is to let the other party know that you are unwilling to participate in further negotiations—and you need an answer, yes or no. This story from Ron Tarrant, the CEO of an international industrial company, illustrates the point:

Ron's company worked for days to submit a million-dollar bid for electrical materials to a contractor who was building a dental school. Ron knew that this particular contractor would typically send Ron's bid to his competitors and tell them, "Beat it, if you can." Of course, someone will always find a way to undercut the previous bid by a few dollars.

This time Ron decided to take a risk. On the day he presented to the contractor, he respectfully described the hard work and research that had gone into the bid, and the total value his company could provide. Ron assured the contractor that his company was ready to go and that the price was more than fair. Finally, he firmly but politely informed the contractor that it was an evaporating price.

"When I leave the office today," said Ron, "this price and proposal leaves with me. We value our relationship with you, and we don't want all our hard work for you to be nitpicked by competitors who haven't done their homework, as we have."

The contractor appreciated Ron's candor, weighed the options, and placed the order that day.

LESSONS LEARNED

- *Be willing to risk. Fair is fair—stand by it.*
- *Be willing to let go if you're not treated fairly.*
- *There are more constructive ways to say, "Take it or leave it."*

WHAT'S MY DISCOUNT?

*If you can't be the
low-priced provider, make it clear that
you're the high-value provider.*

—*Don Galer*

When clients appeal for a discount, it's not always easy to say no, especially if your competitors are willing to cut their prices. If your competitors can do it, why can't you?

I like the way Ron Butler handles it. Ron is the President of an employment service company that does business with thousands of clients and is routinely asked to discount fees.

Example: "The CFO of a regional construction company called to say they wanted to hire a construction site accountant we had referred to them. However, they did not have the $10,000 fee in their budget and requested that we discount the fee because most of our competitors would.

"I think most people can't really appreciate what goes into our service, so I always see this as an opportunity to enhance their awareness. I quickly reviewed the critical steps we take before we refer a candidate, including locating, testing, interviewing, referencing and background checks. I explained that the only way we could discount the fee was to eliminate one or more of the steps in our process, which would make the value of our service hard to justify at any price.

Result: The client thanked me for the explanation, gained a deeper appreciation of the value we provide, and found a way to work our fee into his budget."

Some people request a discount simply because they often get one simply by asking. But others have legitimate concerns about what they're buying and where the value lies. Patiently help them perceive the value; perception is reality.

LESSONS LEARNED

- *Value is the sum total of your package.*
- *Price is only one aspect of that package.*
- *Anticipate discount requests; be prepared to respond clearly and fully.*

CREATIVE FINANCING

Money never starts an idea;
it is the idea that starts the money.

—*W.J. Cameron*

A friend tied up two lakefront lots by borrowing the $7,500 earnest money. She quickly found a second party who agreed to purchase one lot from her at closing—but she insisted he pay the entire down payment for *both* pieces. After all, it was her idea. With no cash outlay, she got her lot and paid back the earnest money—plus earned a tidy profit on the other lot.

A similar story: Pat O'Day made the Rock and Roll Hall of Fame as a disc jockey and promoter. Negotiating appearance contracts with Sixties rock bands required unique skills. In 1963 Pat heard that one band was going to demand a big increase to re-sign. Pat couldn't pay it, so he found a way to have other promoters (his competitors!) pay it.

"I knew this band wanted a new Hammond organ with big speakers," recalls Pat. "I beat the brush and found a great price and terms for that organ. When the musicians demanded their fee increase, I responded, 'Look, guys, you deserve your price. The truth is, I can't pay it, but I may have a better idea. You know that Hammond organ you've been wanting? Wouldn't that help your sound and allow you to raise your rates to other promoters?' They were floored by the question and quickly agreed it was true.

"I said, 'Look, this season's attendance looks thin for me, but I will give you the Hammond if you will waive your fee increases. You can easily turn right around and charge the other promoters your new rate, based on your improved sound system.' They immediately agreed."

LESSONS LEARNED

- *Creativity is as good as cash, sometimes better.*
- *Ideas are scarce; money is plentiful.*
- *Fill a need and the money appears.*

QUESTIONS

Always look for the second right answer.
—Roger von Oech

What people "say" during a negotiation is not nearly as important as what they "mean." They may "say" that the price is absolutely, positively non-negotiable—but they may "mean" that an all-cash deal is the only way they would ever bargain on price. Always search for the second right answer. And the best way to uncover that answer is to ask lots of questions.

Among the best all-purpose questions are simply, "How do you mean?" and "Can you give me an example?" But experienced negotiators often devote many hours to formulating specific questions that are designed to elicit the real underlying interests from the other party. My friend Gary Jacobson, a practicing attorney for more than thirty years, specializes in helping his clients buy or sell their business. His rule of thumb is to average five hours of preparation for every hour of further discovery and negotiation.

Gary gave me a terrific example of the difference between what someone says and what they mean: "If you ask most business owners to disclose their top goal for selling their business, they will almost always answer, 'To get the highest price.' But if you probe deeper, you'll discover that their real underlying concern is to ensure that the person who buys their business actually comes through with the payment. Their stated position is 'top dollar,' but their underlying concern is 'safety and security.'"

If you thoroughly prepare on the front end. . .if you ask lots of good questions. . .if you clarify everyone's underlying interests and expectations. . .then the negotiation process will always go much smoother on the back end.

LESSONS LEARNED

- *Research your subject; never assume anything.*
- *List the questions you plan to ask in advance.*
- *Keep probing ("please explain…can you give me an example") until you arrive at the real concern.*

GOODWILL GESTURES

*Goodwill is the mightiest practical force
in the sales and service universe.*

—*Cat Lane*

Whenever an attorney or a go-between enters a negotiation, a degree of distance is inevitably created between the buyer and the seller. Distance has a way of eroding goodwill. Nowhere is this more evident than in the real estate industry.

Negotiating a house sale can be difficult, first because of the emotional ties sellers have to their homes. Second, because a seller often feels abused after an inspection report comes in. And third, because an agent and/or an attorney are usually in the middle.

True story: Recently, a string of offers and counteroffers over a million-dollar home made the seller wonder if the buyer really wanted the house or was trying to end the transaction. The buyer, a very seasoned negotiator, moved quickly to close the distance by sending his third counteroffer with a gesture of courtesy. He simply instructed his attorney and his agent to inform the sellers that he and his wife both loved the home, that they valued their relationship with the sellers, and that they hoped the sellers would "accept this goodwill gesture in the spirit in which it was offered."

These simple words of assurance softened the edges of the subsequent negotiations and made for a smooth transaction as the final details of the sale were completed over the next several weeks. In most situations, the moment you reach out your hand to the other party, you have closed the distance.

LESSONS LEARNED

- *Distance alone can erode goodwill.*
- *Don't be afraid to reach out.*
- *Common courtesy bridges the gap.*
- *Words do make a difference.*

EXPLORE

Those who wander are not necessarily lost.
—*Kobi Yamada*

We are often told that the shortest distance between two points is a direct line, but that old maxim may not apply in a difficult negotiation. Here's a real world example:

A client of mine, Jack Sparacio, is the CEO of a relatively small firm that manufactures high quality commercial ovens. Recently Jack was approached by one of the world's largest fast food chains and asked to bid on the manufacture of 5,000 custom designed ovens—an exciting opportunity. After several rounds of negotiation, however, it appeared that the opportunity might evaporate. The national chain had reached the absolute limit of its budget constraints, and Jack's firm certainly wasn't willing to deliver the contract at a loss.

At that point, Jack wandered off the beaten track and asked the equivalent of the following question: "Forget ovens for a second. As a company, what is your biggest problem or concern?"

To which the national chain responded with the equivalent of, "We have no idea what that question has to do with ovens, but our biggest concern is probably turnover. Every three weeks we have to re-train someone who is replacing someone who just quit."

To which Jack responded, "What if we could computerize our convection ovens, and program them so that new people only needed to pull the food out at the sound of the buzzer? It may cost a little more than you've budgeted, but those costs should easily be offset by decreases in your training costs." To which the national chain responded, "Why didn't we think of that?"

The result was the biggest order ever for Jack's little company.

LESSONS LEARNED:

- *Negotiation is like a game of "connect the dots."*
- *If there are not enough dots, explore and find new ones.*
- *New dots, new connections, new picture.*

COMPASS POINTS

We can do more than work, we can grow.
—*Suzanne Hoonan*

1. The 5 most important ideas I gained from this book:

_____

_____

_____

2. Specific techniques, ideas, skills or strategies I will
   develop and put into practice:

_____

_____

_____

3. If I do nothing else but apply the value received from
   one lesson, that lesson is:

_____

_____

_____

**CONFLICT IS RESOLVED
NOT THROUGH COMPROMISE,
BUT THROUGH INVENTION.**

- MARY PARKER FOLLETT

ABOUT ADVANTAGE LEARNING SERVICES

ALS is a Seattle based training and consulting firm formed to assist companies and their employees in achieving greater levels of performance and effectiveness.

Over the past 20 years ALS has developed and continues to offer in-depth seminars in the following areas:
• Leadership • Team Development • Attitude Development • Sales Management • Change Management • Sales • Service
• Presentation • Negotiation

ALS has a national account base, many of which participate in their certified train-the-trainer programs. The following is a partial list of our clients:

AT&T	Coca-Cola USA	Weyerhaeuser
Micron	Qwest	I.B.M.
Bank of America	Discover Card	Xerox
Microsoft	U.S. Bank	Lucent
Boeing	Hospital Corp. of	
Nike	America	

Other published products offered by Advantage Learning Services:

"Lessons Learned" Personal Library Series:
I. Sales. II. Service. III. Presentation. IV. Negotiation

Audio/CD/Video/DVD Programs:
• *Increasing Human Effectiveness* • *Team Development*
• *Assessments and Cultural Audits*